TO:

_____

FROM:

_____

DATE:

_____

This is the confidence we have before him:
If we ask anything according to his will, he hears us.
~Isaiah 41:10~

Date: _____

Praises

_____
_____
_____
_____
_____
_____
_____
_____
_____
_____
_____
_____
_____
_____
_____
_____
_____

Confessions

_____
_____
_____
_____
_____
_____
_____
_____
_____
_____
_____
_____
_____
_____
_____
_____

Requests

Answers

Date: _____

Praises

_____
_____
_____
_____
_____
_____
_____
_____
_____
_____
_____
_____
_____
_____
_____
_____
_____

Confessions

_____
_____
_____
_____
_____
_____
_____
_____
_____
_____
_____
_____
_____
_____
_____
_____

Requests

Answers

Date: _____

Praises

_____
_____
_____
_____
_____
_____
_____
_____
_____
_____
_____
_____
_____
_____
_____
_____

Confessions

_____
_____
_____
_____
_____
_____
_____
_____
_____
_____
_____
_____
_____
_____
_____
_____
_____

Requests

Answers

Date: _____

Praises

_____
_____
_____
_____
_____
_____
_____
_____
_____
_____
_____
_____
_____
_____
_____
_____

Confessions

_____
_____
_____
_____
_____
_____
_____
_____
_____
_____
_____
_____
_____
_____
_____
_____

Requests

Answers

Date: _____

Praises

_____
_____
_____
_____
_____
_____
_____
_____
_____
_____
_____
_____
_____

Confessions

_____
_____
_____
_____
_____
_____
_____
_____
_____
_____
_____
_____
_____
_____

Requests

Answers

Date: _____

Praises

_____
_____
_____
_____
_____
_____
_____
_____
_____
_____
_____
_____
_____
_____
_____

Confessions

_____
_____
_____
_____
_____
_____
_____
_____
_____
_____
_____
_____
_____
_____
_____
_____
_____

Requests

Answers

Date: _____

Praises

_____
_____
_____
_____
_____
_____
_____
_____
_____
_____
_____
_____
_____
_____
_____
_____

Confessions

_____
_____
_____
_____
_____
_____
_____
_____
_____
_____
_____
_____
_____
_____
_____
_____
_____

Requests

Answers

Date: _____

Praises

_____

_____
_____
_____
_____
_____
_____
_____
_____
_____
_____
_____
_____

Confessions

_____
_____
_____
_____
_____
_____
_____
_____
_____
_____
_____
_____
_____
_____
_____
_____

Requests

Answers

Date: _____

Praises

_____
_____
_____
_____
_____
_____
_____
_____
_____
_____
_____
_____
_____
_____
_____

Confessions

_____
_____
_____
_____
_____
_____
_____
_____
_____
_____
_____
_____
_____
_____
_____
_____

Requests

Answers

Date: _____

Praises

_____
_____
_____
_____
_____
_____
_____
_____
_____
_____
_____
_____
_____
_____
_____

Confessions

_____
_____
_____
_____
_____
_____
_____
_____
_____
_____
_____
_____
_____
_____
_____
_____
_____

Requests

Answers

Date: _____

Praises

_____
_____
_____
_____
_____
_____
_____
_____
_____
_____
_____
_____
_____

Confessions

_____
_____
_____
_____
_____
_____
_____
_____
_____
_____
_____
_____
_____
_____

Requests

Answers

Date: _____

Praises

_____

_____
_____
_____
_____
_____
_____
_____
_____
_____
_____
_____
_____
_____
_____
_____

Confessions

_____
_____
_____
_____
_____
_____
_____
_____
_____
_____
_____
_____
_____
_____
_____
_____
_____

Requests

Answers

Date: _____

Praises

_____
_____
_____
_____
_____
_____
_____
_____
_____
_____
_____
_____
_____
_____
_____

Confessions

_____
_____
_____
_____
_____
_____
_____
_____
_____
_____
_____
_____
_____
_____
_____
_____
_____

Requests

Answers

Date: _____

Praises

_____
_____
_____
_____
_____
_____
_____
_____
_____
_____
_____
_____
_____
_____

Confessions

_____
_____
_____
_____
_____
_____
_____
_____
_____
_____
_____
_____
_____
_____
_____
_____
_____

Requests

Answers

Date: _____

Praises

_____
_____
_____
_____
_____
_____
_____
_____
_____
_____
_____
_____
_____
_____
_____

Confessions

_____
_____
_____
_____
_____
_____
_____
_____
_____
_____
_____
_____
_____
_____
_____
_____

Requests

Answers

Date: _____

Praises

_____
_____
_____
_____
_____
_____
_____
_____
_____
_____
_____
_____
_____

Confessions

_____
_____
_____
_____
_____
_____
_____
_____
_____
_____
_____
_____
_____
_____
_____

Requests

Answers

Date: _____

Praises

_____
_____
_____
_____
_____
_____
_____
_____
_____
_____
_____
_____
_____
_____

Confessions

_____
_____
_____
_____
_____
_____
_____
_____
_____
_____
_____
_____
_____
_____

Requests

Answers

Date: _____

Praises

_____
_____
_____
_____
_____
_____
_____
_____
_____
_____
_____
_____
_____

Confessions

_____
_____
_____
_____
_____
_____
_____
_____
_____
_____
_____
_____
_____
_____
_____

Requests

Answers

Date: _____

Praises

_____
_____
_____
_____
_____
_____
_____
_____
_____
_____
_____
_____
_____

Confessions

_____
_____
_____
_____
_____
_____
_____
_____
_____
_____
_____
_____
_____
_____

Requests

Answers

Date: _____

Praises

_____
_____
_____
_____
_____
_____
_____
_____
_____
_____
_____
_____
_____
_____

Confessions

_____
_____
_____
_____
_____
_____
_____
_____
_____
_____
_____
_____
_____
_____
_____

Requests

Answers

Date: _____

Praises

_____
_____
_____
_____
_____
_____
_____
_____
_____
_____
_____
_____
_____
_____
_____

Confessions

_____
_____
_____
_____
_____
_____
_____
_____
_____
_____
_____
_____
_____
_____
_____

Requests

Answers

Date: _____

Praises

_____
_____
_____
_____
_____
_____
_____
_____
_____
_____
_____
_____
_____

Confessions

_____
_____
_____
_____
_____
_____
_____
_____
_____
_____
_____
_____
_____
_____
_____
_____

Requests

Answers

Date: _____

Praises

Confessions

Requests

Answers

Date: _____

Praises

_____
_____
_____
_____
_____
_____
_____
_____
_____
_____
_____
_____
_____

Confessions

_____
_____
_____
_____
_____
_____
_____
_____
_____
_____
_____
_____
_____
_____
_____

Requests

Answers

Date: _____

Praises

_____
_____
_____
_____
_____
_____
_____
_____
_____
_____
_____
_____
_____
_____
_____
_____

Confessions

_____
_____
_____
_____
_____
_____
_____
_____
_____
_____
_____
_____
_____
_____
_____
_____
_____

Requests

Answers

Date: _____

Praises

_____
_____
_____
_____
_____
_____
_____
_____
_____
_____
_____
_____
_____
_____

Confessions

_____
_____
_____
_____
_____
_____
_____
_____
_____
_____
_____
_____
_____
_____
_____
_____

Requests

Answers

Date: _____

Praises

_____
_____
_____
_____
_____
_____
_____
_____
_____
_____
_____
_____
_____
_____
_____
_____

Confessions

_____
_____
_____
_____
_____
_____
_____
_____
_____
_____
_____
_____
_____
_____
_____
_____

Requests

Answers

Date: _____

Praises

_____
_____
_____
_____
_____
_____
_____
_____
_____
_____
_____
_____
_____
_____

Confessions

_____
_____
_____
_____
_____
_____
_____
_____
_____
_____
_____
_____
_____

Requests

Answers

Date: _____

Praises

Confessions

Requests

Answers

Date: _____

Praises

_____
_____
_____
_____
_____
_____
_____
_____
_____
_____
_____
_____
_____
_____

Confessions

_____
_____
_____
_____
_____
_____
_____
_____
_____
_____
_____
_____
_____
_____
_____
_____
_____

Requests

Answers

Date: _____

Praises

_____
_____
_____
_____
_____
_____
_____
_____
_____
_____
_____
_____
_____
_____
_____

Confessions

_____
_____
_____
_____
_____
_____
_____
_____
_____
_____
_____
_____
_____
_____
_____
_____

Requests

Answers

Date: _____

Praises

_____
_____
_____
_____
_____
_____
_____
_____
_____
_____
_____
_____
_____
_____
_____

Confessions

_____
_____
_____
_____
_____
_____
_____
_____
_____
_____
_____
_____
_____
_____
_____
_____

Requests

Answers

Date: _____

Praises

_____
_____
_____
_____
_____
_____
_____
_____
_____
_____
_____
_____
_____
_____
_____

Confessions

_____
_____
_____
_____
_____
_____
_____
_____
_____
_____
_____
_____
_____
_____
_____
_____

Requests

Answers

Date: _____

Praises

_____
_____
_____
_____
_____
_____
_____
_____
_____
_____
_____
_____
_____
_____

Confessions

Requests

Answers

Date: _____

Praises

_____
_____
_____
_____
_____
_____
_____
_____
_____
_____
_____
_____
_____
_____
_____

Confessions

_____
_____
_____
_____
_____
_____
_____
_____
_____
_____
_____
_____
_____
_____
_____
_____
_____

Requests

Answers

Date: _____

Praises

_____
_____
_____
_____
_____
_____
_____
_____
_____
_____
_____
_____
_____

Confessions

_____
_____
_____
_____
_____
_____
_____
_____
_____
_____
_____
_____
_____

Requests

Answers

Date: _____

Praises

_____
_____
_____
_____
_____
_____
_____
_____
_____
_____
_____
_____
_____
_____
_____

Confessions

_____
_____
_____
_____
_____
_____
_____
_____
_____
_____
_____
_____
_____
_____
_____
_____
_____

Requests

Answers

Date: _____

Praises

_____
_____
_____
_____
_____
_____
_____
_____
_____
_____
_____
_____
_____
_____
_____
_____

Confessions

_____
_____
_____
_____
_____
_____
_____
_____
_____
_____
_____
_____
_____
_____
_____

Requests

Answers

Date: _____

Praises

_____
_____
_____
_____
_____
_____
_____
_____
_____
_____
_____
_____
_____
_____

Confessions

_____
_____
_____
_____
_____
_____
_____
_____
_____
_____
_____
_____
_____
_____
_____
_____

Requests

Answers

Date: _____

Praises

Confessions

Requests

Answers

Date: _____

Praises

_____
_____
_____
_____
_____
_____
_____
_____
_____
_____
_____
_____
_____
_____

Confessions

_____
_____
_____
_____
_____
_____
_____
_____
_____
_____
_____
_____
_____
_____

Requests

Answers

Date: _____

Praises

Confessions

Requests

Answers

Date: _____

Praises

_____

_____
_____
_____
_____
_____
_____
_____
_____
_____
_____
_____
_____

Confessions

_____
_____
_____
_____
_____
_____
_____
_____
_____
_____
_____
_____
_____
_____

Requests

Answers

Date: _____

Praises

_____
_____
_____
_____
_____
_____
_____
_____
_____
_____
_____
_____
_____
_____
_____
_____

Confessions

_____
_____
_____
_____
_____
_____
_____
_____
_____
_____
_____
_____
_____
_____
_____
_____

Requests

Answers

Date: _____

Praises

Confessions

Requests

Answers

Date: _____

Praises

_____
_____
_____
_____
_____
_____
_____
_____
_____
_____
_____
_____
_____
_____

Confessions

_____
_____
_____
_____
_____
_____
_____
_____
_____
_____
_____
_____
_____
_____
_____
_____

Requests

Answers

Date: _____

Praises

_____
_____
_____
_____
_____
_____
_____
_____
_____
_____
_____
_____
_____
_____
_____
_____

Confessions

_____
_____
_____
_____
_____
_____
_____
_____
_____
_____
_____
_____
_____
_____
_____
_____

Requests

Answers

Date: _____

Praises

_____
_____
_____
_____
_____
_____
_____
_____
_____
_____
_____
_____
_____
_____

Confessions

_____
_____
_____
_____
_____
_____
_____
_____
_____
_____
_____
_____
_____
_____

Requests

Answers

Date: _____

Praises

_____
_____
_____
_____
_____
_____
_____
_____
_____
_____
_____
_____
_____
_____

Confessions

_____
_____
_____
_____
_____
_____
_____
_____
_____
_____
_____
_____
_____
_____
_____
_____

Requests

Answers

Date: _____

Praises

_____
_____
_____
_____
_____
_____
_____
_____
_____
_____
_____
_____
_____
_____

Confessions

_____
_____
_____
_____
_____
_____
_____
_____
_____
_____
_____
_____
_____
_____
_____

Requests

Answers

Date: _____

Praises

_____
_____
_____
_____
_____
_____
_____
_____
_____
_____
_____
_____
_____
_____
_____

Confessions

_____
_____
_____
_____
_____
_____
_____
_____
_____
_____
_____
_____
_____
_____
_____
_____

Requests

Answers

Date: _____

Praises

Confessions

Requests

Answers

Date: _____

Praises

_____
_____
_____
_____
_____
_____
_____
_____
_____
_____
_____
_____
_____
_____

Confessions

_____
_____
_____
_____
_____
_____
_____
_____
_____
_____
_____
_____
_____
_____
_____

Requests

Answers

Date: _____

Praises

Confessions

Requests

Answers

Date: _____

Praises

Confessions

Requests

Answers

Date: _____

Praises

_____

_____

_____

_____

_____

_____

_____

_____

_____

_____

_____

_____

_____

_____

_____

_____

_____

Confessions

_____

_____

_____

_____

_____

_____

_____

_____

_____

_____

_____

_____

_____

_____

_____

_____

_____

Requests

Answers

Date: _____

Praises

_____
_____
_____
_____
_____
_____
_____
_____
_____
_____
_____
_____
_____
_____
_____
_____
_____

Confessions

_____
_____
_____
_____
_____
_____
_____
_____
_____
_____
_____
_____
_____
_____
_____
_____
_____
_____

Requests

Answers

Date: _____

Praises

_____
_____
_____
_____
_____
_____
_____
_____
_____
_____
_____
_____
_____
_____
_____
_____

Confessions

_____
_____
_____
_____
_____
_____
_____
_____
_____
_____
_____
_____
_____
_____
_____
_____
_____

Requests

Answers

Date: _____

Praises

_____
_____
_____
_____
_____
_____
_____
_____
_____
_____
_____
_____
_____
_____
_____
_____
_____

Confessions

_____
_____
_____
_____
_____
_____
_____
_____
_____
_____
_____
_____
_____
_____
_____
_____
_____

Requests

Answers

Date: _____

Praises

_____
_____
_____
_____
_____
_____
_____
_____
_____
_____
_____
_____
_____
_____
_____
_____

Confessions

_____
_____
_____
_____
_____
_____
_____
_____
_____
_____
_____
_____
_____
_____
_____
_____
_____

Requests

Answers

Date: _____

Praises

_____
_____
_____
_____
_____
_____
_____
_____
_____
_____
_____
_____
_____
_____
_____
_____

Confessions

_____
_____
_____
_____
_____
_____
_____
_____
_____
_____
_____
_____
_____
_____
_____
_____
_____
_____

Requests

Answers

Date: _____

Praises

_____
_____
_____
_____
_____
_____
_____
_____
_____
_____
_____
_____
_____
_____
_____
_____

Confessions

_____
_____
_____
_____
_____
_____
_____
_____
_____
_____
_____
_____
_____
_____
_____
_____

Requests

Answers